NEW JERSEY
Naturescapes & Detail

WALTER CHOROSZEWSKI

Introduction By JOHN CUNNINGHAM

Published by AESTHETIC PRESS, INC., Somerville, NJ

WALTER CHOROSZEWSKI

As a photographer, author, and lecturer, Walter Choroszewski has been enhancing the image of New Jersey through his many photographic books and calendars since 1981. Choroszewski's photography is widely published both editorially and commercially, and his fine art prints appear in galleries and many corporate collections. Walter, with his wife, Susan, and son, Joe, live in Somerset County.

JOHN CUNNINGHAM

Best known for his lifelong dedication to writing about New Jersey, John Cunningham's career in journalism began with the *Morristown Record*, followed by notable years with the *Newark News*. Cunningham has published over 20 books about the state, including high school and elementary texts. "Mr. New Jersey," a title given him by Rutgers University, is most fitting for the state's leading advocate of New Jersey Pride. John and his wife, Dorothy, are long-time residents of Morris County.

Dedicated with love to Susan and Joe

NEW JERSEY, Naturescapes & Detail

Copyright © 1992 by Aesthetic Press, Inc.
Photography & Text - Copyright © 1992 by Walter Choroszewski
Introduction - Copyright ©1992 by John Cunningham

Softcover Edition - 1992
Hardcover Edition - 1995
Second Printing - 1998
Printed in Korea
International Standard Book Number 0-933605-05-6
Library of Congress Catalog Card Number 92-070484

Published by

AESTHETIC PRESS, INC.
PO Box 5306, North Branch Station
Somerville, NJ 08876-1303

Right: A summer sunrise on Lake Oswego at Penn State Forest.

4

INTRODUCTION

By

JOHN CUNNINGHAM

Left: Pink and white dogwood at Frelinghuysen Arboretum, Morristown.

Inset: Morning dew sparkles the grass at Liberty State Park.

In the beginning, after the last of the glaciers loosened its icy hold on the northern part of the globe and retreated northward 40,000 years ago, the land that would be called New Jersey had emerged — a place of mountains and seashore, rolling hills and varied forestlands, two broad rivers that shaped borders, and inland streams that both drained and replenished the earth.

Animals roamed the woods, drank their fill at clean waterways, and grew sleek on the ample natural food supply. These were beasts as large as mastodons, the last of the mighty prehistoric behemoths. Sharing the terrain were animals as varied as elk, wolves, otters, foxes, racoons, deer, and squirrels. Warblers, woodpeckers and flickers filled the forests with song. Flowers brightened the landscape, from dogwood blossoming in the Piedmont to exotic plants flourishing in the sandy soil of what human beings eventually would call the Pine Barrens.

If doomsayers are to be believed, all of the once-pristine land and its flora and fauna have disappeared under the laying of cement, the proliferation of cities, and the spread of humans in what sociological jargon smugly calls "urban sprawl." The most pessimistic of people moan that the best is gone. Optimists counter there is much yet to be cherished.

Walter Choroszewski is among the optimistic, and with far more reason than naive faith or chauvinistic pride. His travels through every corner of New Jersey have shown him ample evidence of a terrain similar to what "used to be."

This book amply documents the point. It is not a guide book, a history of nature, or "just for pretty" decoration. It loosens such straitjackets of thought, asking only that the viewers imagine themselves gazing upon the familiar landscape for the first time.

Do not seek within these pages fine architectural renderings, people tilling the fields, or church spires reaching skyward. Such evidences of human presence have been

deliberately set aside for the more eternal virtues of the land and its bounties. None of man's conceits is more noble than one of the great trees that were saplings before the first Europeans debarked on this shore. Human works of art pale in contrast with nature's plumage.

Return in these pages to an intriguing documentation of the landscape as it might have been when mastodons roamed, when the Great Swamp and magnificent Falls of the Passaic came to be, and when humans discovered and settled the land between the Kittatinny Mountains on the north and the broad Delaware Bay 166 miles to the south. Return to formations of rock cast by ancient volcanoes, to when plunging waterfalls were but trickles of water, and to when flora and fauna settled into a natural progression.

To see one's world as nature planned it is to experience some of the awe that must have overwhelmed the area's first settlers about 10,000 years ago. They were a nomadic people, homeless until they reached their dream of a golden sun shining through mists swirling above the Atlantic Ocean. These were American Indians, New Jersey's first immigrants as well as its first settlers.

They had traveled from halfway around the world, wandering eastward for thousands of years after forsaking the cold plains of what is now Siberia. On the sands that would become known as the Jersey Shore, they experienced what has been described in a noted Indian legend as "the sunrise . . . a rich land, a pleasant land."

Left: Trunk detail of an ancient Swamp Oak in Burlington County.

Inset: The lush Tillman Ravine in Stokes State Forest.

No one can truly depict in words or photographs the emotions of those first humans who gazed upon the Atlantic, or walked over the Kittatinny Mountains, to stalk game in the Pine Barrens. But in seeking "the natural," Walter Choroszewski offers at least a chance to sense thoughts of a peaceful people in tune with the land.

Can the basic reactions of an almost-vanished culture be imagined? Of course; we experience such reactions in our daily lives. Who has not felt both joy and awe in watching ocean waves tumble endlessly on a white sand beach? Who can scramble over the dunes of Island Beach for the first time without sensing some of the excitement that enthralls strangers in a new land? Who has not felt privileged at finding a rare flower in the Pine Barrens, or watching white-tailed deer bound into a Highlands thicket?

Finding the land of long ago requires a sense of written history to recall how the first explorers and first colonists described the eastern boundary of the region that would be called New Jersey. The first European to sail within New Jersey waters and to describe them (albeit briefly) was Giovanni da Verrazano, an Italian captain sailing for France. In 1524, he dropped anchor in what English settlers in time named Newark Bay. Then he ventured northward on what he termed "una grandissima riviera." That poetic appreciation later was abandoned for the workday, unsentimental, "Hudson River." Verrazano's journey up river led to his discovery of the magnificent and lofty Palisades, which the impressionable Italian navigator saw as an impregnable guardian of the grandissima riviera that flowed beneath its base.

The Palisades are a solid reminder of prehistory; they were formed by an ancient volcano located near present-day Boonton. To see them is to know some of the way this part of the world has been for 100 million years. The landmark survives, much as it was when explorer Henry Hudson saw it in 1609: "A cliffe, that looked the colour of white greene, as though it were either a copper or silver myne."

Inset: White tails of deer flash by at Voorhees State Park.

Right: Ocean vista at Deal, Monmouth County.

The 1609 description of the Palisades actually was written by Robert Juet, mate

aboard Hudson's HALF MOON. Juet's entries on the Jersey shore also offer to us an illuminating guide to the coast as it appeared 400 years ago. Remarkably, it could be a rough chart for today.

The mate described "a great bay" (The Delaware Bay), "full of shoalds" off the tip of Cape May. As the HALF MOON coasted northward, Juet noted "the bodie of Ilands" ranged parallel to the mainland — the barrier islands still in place between Cape May and Island Beach. Juet also mentions a "great lake of water" (Barnegat Bay), and its mouth, Barnegat Inlet, where, in Juet's words, "the sea breaketh on the shoalds."

Much to the pleasure of seaside publicists in any time, the English logkeeper also wrote a line that all Jersey Shore promoters insist was penned to define their section of the strand: "A very good land to fall with, and a pleasant land to see." A pleasant land to see —a land of dunes and beach plums, of stretches of lonely sand, of centuries-old holly trees and ever-recurring bayberry bushes.

Inland, deep in the pine woodland called barren by colonists because it failed to favor traditional crops, there are secret places where wild orchids thrive (at least 25 varieties of them) along with fringed gentians, bog asphodel, pitcher plants that trap insects for food, and another 400 or so flowering plants. Barren indeed!

Left: The towering cliffs of the Palisades in Bergen County.

Inset: The solitary dunes on the shore of Island Beach State Park.

Dare we imagine Indian or colonial families plucking bouquets of these exotic flowers as they trekked through the pine forests? Why not; it would be as natural as walking. Today's conservationists agonize at the very thought of picking a wild orchid (much less transplanting one), but a camera in skilled hands can leave the wildflowers in place, yet bring them out of their natural habitat for all to know and enjoy.

Just as we are being asked to imagine the Pine Barrens of long ago, we can envision being the first to see the vast hardwood forests that shade northwestern New Jersey and spill over as far as the eye can see into New York State and Pennsylvania. The New Jersey portion of the woodland stretches slightly southwestward along this ridge.

The Appalachian Trail follows that spine of the Kittatinny Ridge all the way to the Delaware Water Gap, a prime example of nature's unending battle between water and rock, always won by water no matter how long the battle lasts. Indians stood in awe of the mysterious gap and 19th century travelers rode carriages and trains out to see the natural wonder. It is still a compelling sight.

Unblemished spring-fed Kittatinny Mountain lakes are easily reached from the Appalachian Trail. In season, a bear may be encountered, a bobcat may yowl in the darkness, or an Eastern Coyote might lope across the trail. Often in summer rattlesnakes sun themselves on warm rocks beside the path. This is wild country, still resistant to permanent human encroachment.

The Kittatinny Mountains are the stuff of geological violence, the very kind of solid base on which all of the world rests. Once, according to one school of geological thought, the mountains of New Jersey rose to heights of 30,000 feet, as towering as the modern Himalayas. The surface of the earth buckled and folded, rose and fell, a turbulence clearly demonstrated in the road cut through the Delaware Water Gap.

A particularly pleasant perch on the Kittatinnys is at Sunrise Mountain, both for the view eastward to the placid Highlands and for its easy accessibility. Below,

Inset: Spring green returns to the forest near High Point.

Right: Fog shrouds the awesome Delaware Water Gap.

is the Kittatinny Valley. Beyond, the Highlands roll eastward, ever diminishing in a meander toward sea level. Highlands is not a fancy real estate developer's designation or a catchword for environmentalists struggling to preserve at least a bit of this splendid land of forests and fresh water lakes. It is a physiographic term for the oldest geological part of New Jersey.

A surprising sight in the Highlands is one of the increasing flocks of wild turkeys returning to the area where they rightfully belong, after an absence of several decades. In the forests, too, mountain laurel flourishes in late spring. Blazing foliage and wildflower fields brighten the Highlands in autumn.

The Highlands blend easily into the Piedmont, although the merger is somewhat obscured by the Watchung Mountains, remnant of lava flows that swept across the land a hundred million years ago. Today the Watchungs serenely range from Paterson south to Bound Brook, then swing sharply to the north-west toward Pluckemin. The ridges became doubly important in history.

For one thing, the Watchungs formed the eastern barrier for prehistoric Lake Passaic, thirty miles long and ten miles wide, whose draining about 40,000 years ago left behind the Great Swamp. For another thing, the Watchungs created a perfect barrier and lookout point for George Washington when twice he led his army into Morristown.

The violence of long ago made possible the natural serenity of today. It laid down the rich soil in which the great hardwood forests of the north flourish. It created an

Left Inset: A radiant field of tickweed shines in Bedminster.

Right Inset: Cape May "Diamonds" on the beach of Cape May Point.

exact mix of nutrients in sandy soil that enables a tremendous number of wild plants to flourish in the Pine Barrens.

Violence reared up the mountains, leveled the plains, and gouged out lake beds. It created the waterfalls, the riverbeds, the Palisades, and broad marshes. Nature was bountiful and whimsical in laying down the base for New Jersey — whimsical even to the point of filling Delaware Bay with huge chunks of quartz that each day yield small shining pieces to the beach at Cape May Point. Humans who find the bits of quartz call them "Cape May diamonds."

Treasure is in the beholder's eye. Settle back. Turn the pages slowly. You are about to enter a natural world. Share in the treasures of Walter Choroszewski's natural vision of New Jersey.

Left: Sleepy geese rest
on a Kittatinny Mountain
lake near Peters Valley.

Inset: Downy goslings
born at Edwin B. Forsythe
National Wildlife Refuge.

Right: Canada geese
feed on the duckweed at
Waterloo Village.

PROLOGUE

By
WALTER
CHOROSZEWSKI

Left: A lush waterway near the Wading River in the Pine Barrens.

Inset: The rare Pine Barrens Gentian, Wharton State Forest.

My first photographic sojourns into New Jersey in 1980 were no surprise to me. I knew that just beyond the urban perimeter of New York City, natural treasures awaited.

From my childhood through college years in Pennsylvania, to my first professional years in New York City, I was quite familiar with the land that fell between. My first memories of New Jersey were of family visits to relatives who lived in the flat and warm climate only a few hours from home. Our summer trips to the Jersey shore were also a special memory, a place where I jumped in the waves, and collected sea shells as souvenirs.

After college my first jobs brought me to New York City. I traversed New Jersey often, with Route 80 as my corridor. I never took for granted the awesome Delaware Water Gap, nor the powerful Palisades that stood guard as I crossed the George Washington Bridge — I often stopped at both for a respectful closer look.

After a few years of photographing the Garden State, I decided to make New Jersey home for my family. We chose the central rolling landscape of Somerset County, with its rivers, fields, and forest — a pleasant change from NYC.

I make my living at showing the positive aspects of life in New Jersey. This photographic collection, with its emphasis on the natural, is my answer to those who believe the cliches and only see the problems.

I have visited every county and present nature's bounty that lies within each. My images show the diversity of the land from the rugged mountains, to the alluring ocean; from the charm of the hills to the mystery of the pinelands. These photos share my appreciation for God's blessing of a land called New Jersey.

*Left: Ridges of
bedrock break the surface
at High Point State Park.*

*Right: Laughing gulls
take flight along the
Delaware Bay.*

Left: Cranberries float
in a bog near Sim Place.

Inset: White pine
silhouette near Atsion.

Right: Wind blown
snow sweeps across
Great Meadows.

Overleaf: Loosestrife
in bloom at Lee Meadows
in Morris County.

Left: Early morning calm
reflected in Echo Lake.

Right: Mountain Laurel
blooms at Skylands Manor
in Ringwood.

Left: Sunset illuminates the phragmites grass at Clarks Pond, Fairton.

Right: Ferns turn to autumn gold along Van Campens Brook, Millbrook.

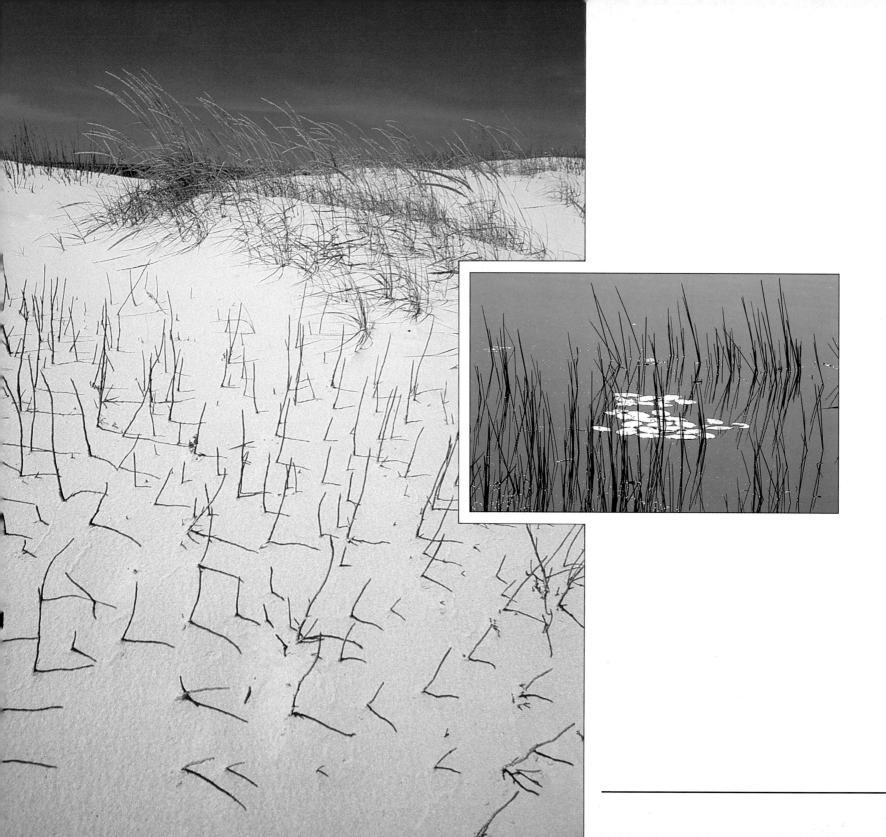

Left: The sand dunes of
Island Beach State Park.

Inset: Shore detail
at Wawayanda Lake.

Right: A foggy morning
along the Breeches Branch
of the Oswego River.

*Left: Sunset glow on
the face of Mt. Tammany.*

*Inset: Cape May dunes
offer rest to migrating
monarch butterflies.*

*Right: Fallen leaves
on a rock shelf at
Little Falls.*

*Left: Frost on a
meadow near Clementon.*

*Right: Ten below
zero at the Great Falls.*

Left: Sunlit tree
against the shadows of
the Delaware Water Gap.

Inset: A pitcher plant
awaits prey at Whitesbog.

Right: The first light
of day raking the lily
pads of Farrington Lake.

Left: Autumn colors
border Diamond Mill
Pond at South Mountain
Reservation.

Right: The powerful
Boonton Falls on the
Rockaway River.

Overleaf: The Ken
Lockwood Gorge on the
South Branch of the
Raritan River.

Left: October's morning
mist rising above the
Lamington River.

Inset: Great blue heron
soars over Carnegie Lake
in Princeton.

42

Right: Forest sunrise at
Lewis Morris County Park.

Left: The spring return
of horseshoe crabs along
the Delaware Bay.

Right: Dawn's light
reflected in Black Brook
at Spruce Run Reservoir.

Left: A gathering of egrets at the Great Bay Wildlife Management Area.

Left Inset: Thousands of migratory shore birds visit Reeds Beach.

Right: Herons, egrets, and ibises share a pond at Brigantine.

Right Inset: Snowy egret hunts the waters of Cold Spring Harbor.

Left: A fresh snowfall
blankets the Raritan
River near Califon.

Right: Peach blossom
detail near Turnersville.

Left: Morning fog
near the confluence of
the Raritan Rivers.

Right: Rainbow mist
bridges the Great Falls.

Inset: Wind-driven art
at the dunes of Avalon.

Left: A rare record
swamp oak flourishes in
Burlington County.

Right: Tree roots cling
to the steep rock face of
Kittatinny Mountain.

Left: Sunset light on
the dunes of Sandy Hook.

Right: Maple leaves
in detail, Sussex County.

Overleaf: The mighty
Atlantic surf crashes
at Sea Bright.

Left: A Kittatinny
Mountain lake in Stokes
State Forest.

Inset: A colorful
male wood duck, Clinton.

Right: Broadleaved
arrowhead thrives in
the Great Swamp.

Left: Clouds rise
from the Delaware River,
as viewed from the
Appalachian Trail.

Right: Ascending
clouds of moisture
above the river at the
Delaware Water Gap.

61

Left: A swallowtail
butterfly found at the
Colonial Park Sensory
Garden, Somerset County.

Inset: A common
yellowthroat sings
in the marshes near
Stone Harbor.

Right: A double
rainbow arches a field
in South Branch.

Left: Rushing waters
of a mountain stream at
Worthington State Forest.

Right: Brilliant foliage
surrounds Speedwell Lake.

Left: A new wet
snow frosts Sunrise
Mountain.

Inset: Winterberry
detail near Jenny Jump
State Forest.

Right: Tranquil Batsto
Lake mirrors the clouds
and sky above.

Left: Fawn in a field of daisies, Somerset County.

Right: Wildflowers bloom at edge of the Great Passaic Falls.

Left: An overnight snow ices the Palisades.

Right: Waves break on the jetties near Belmar.

Overleaf: Predawn glow on a Pine Barrens pond in Penn State Forest.

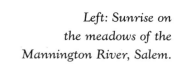

Left: Sunrise on the meadows of the Mannington River, Salem.

Inset: Flocks of Snow Geese arrive at Brigantine.

Right: The peaceful waters of the Edwin B. Forsythe Wildlife Refuge.

Left: Dogwood and spring
wildflowers share a field
in Tewksbury.

Inset: Wild yellow iris
near the Raritan River.

Right: Morning light
breaks along the Delaware
Raritan Canal near
Blackwells Mills.

Left: A tranquil morning on the wetlands near the Maurice River.

Right: Buttermilk Falls cascading down the face of Kittatinny Ridge.

Overleaf: Reflections of autumn in Surprise Lake at Watchung Reservation.

Overleaf Inset: Sunset silhouette, Logan Pond.